Sable Island

The Wandering Sandbar

Wendy Kitts

NIMBUS
PUBLISHING

Nimbus Publishing Limited
3731 Mackintosh St,
Halifax, NS B3K 5A5
(902) 455-4286
nimbus.ca

Printed and bound in Canada

Design: Andrew Herygers

Library and Archives Canada Cataloguing in Publication

Kitts, Wendy
Sable Island : the wandering sandbar / Wendy Kitts.
ISBN 978-1-55109-865-4

1. Sable Island (N.S.)—Juvenile literature. 2. Natural history—Nova Scotia—Sable Island—Juvenile literature. 3. Sable Island (N.S.)—History—Juvenile literature. I. Title.

FC2345.S22K58 2011   j971.6'99   C2011-903915-X

Canada NOVA SCOTIA Communities, Culture and Heritage The Canada Council Le Conseil des Arts for the Arts du Canada

Nimbus Publishing acknowledges the financial support for its publishing activities from the Government of Canada through the Canada Book Fund (CBF) and the Canada Council for the Arts, and from the Province of Nova Scotia through the Department of Communities, Culture and Heritage.

With love to my mother, Alice, who instilled in me the love of both nature and books, and to my friend Wes, who taught me to always say yes to whatever life puts in front of me.

Table of Contents

Introduction

What if I told you that there is a land that once gave pirates a place to hide yet held prisoners captive, where there are more horses than people, and where the sand not only sings but can swallow a ship whole? Where you have to be careful not only of the quicksand, but also of the sharks in the water that surrounds this land?

Would you believe me?

What if I told you that this wild and magical land was in Canada? Would you believe me then?

The horses on Sable Island barely notice humans, unless they get too close to their babies.

This isn't a make-believe land in a bedtime story. This is a real place, and yes, it is in Canada. I know, because I've been there and everything I've just told you...is true.

Sable Island

Sable Island is a tiny **sandbar**[1] in the middle of the Atlantic Ocean. Most people have never heard of it, even though it was discovered almost five hundred years ago. Sable Island looks like any other beautiful beach that you might visit on vacation, but don't let that fool you. When you are on Sable Island, you are in the wild. Hundreds of wild horses and tens of thousands of seals live on Sable Island. They might look friendly, but both will attack you if you get too close to their babies. Sable Island has pinkish sandy beaches along the entire coast of the island, but it's too dangerous to swim there. The waves are strong and there are sharks in the sparkling waters that surround Sable. You even

> *Sable Island looks like any other beautiful beach that you might visit on vacation, but don't let that fool you. When you are on Sable Island, you are in the wild.*

1. Check the Glossary on page 86 for definitions of all the words you see in blue!

have to watch out for quicksand. No, this is no day at the beach.

Sable Island has a wild history full of stories of pirates, ghosts, and hundreds of shipwrecks whose treasures are still buried under the blowing sands. These stories may sound unbelievable, but they are all true.

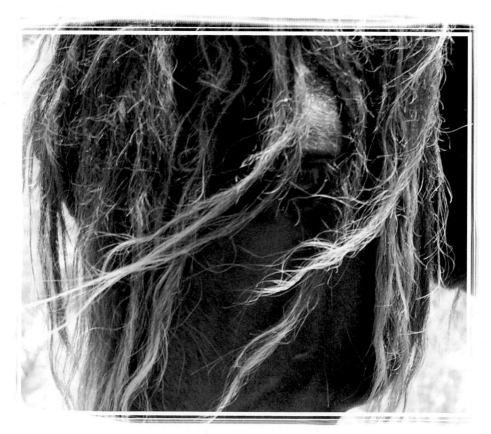

On Sable Island, the horses outnumber the people.

The seals bodysurf on the wild waves that crash onto Sable's shores.

A grey seal sunbathes on the beach.

Even today, Sable Island is a magical place where the sand sings when you walk on it, and wandering sand dunes slowly tiptoe across the island. There is beauty everywhere you look, and wildlife that you won't find anywhere else. You can sit quietly cheek-to-cheek with a curious horse, or laugh at the seals as they bodysurf on the wild ocean waves.

It sounds like a fairy tale, doesn't it?

CHAPTER ONE

The Wandering Sandbar

A Giant Sandbox

Sable Island is a tiny, curved island in the middle of the Atlantic Ocean. It is part of the province of Nova Scotia even though three hundred kilometres of water separate Sable Island from Halifax—that's about the distance between Halifax and Fredericton.

Sable is the French word for sand, and Sable Island is really just a big pile of sand. The sand is forty metres deep. That's about the height of thirty-five children

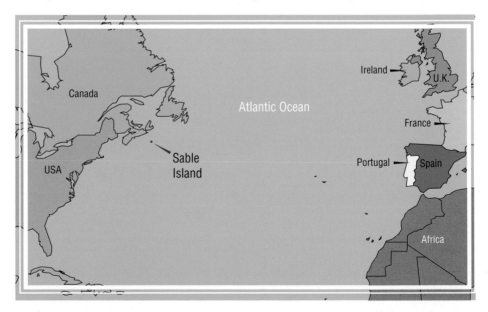

Sable Island is part of Nova Scotia even though they are separated by three hundred kilometres of water.

standing on each other's shoulders. That's a big sandbox!

Scientists think that Sable Island formed during the last ice age, fifteen thousand years ago, when glaciers from the North Pole pushed into what we now call Canada. Glaciers are big sheets of ice, and the edge of the ice is like a giant snowplow pushing the ground in front of it as it spreads. And as this glacier spread, it picked up sand and gravel along the way. The sand and gravel travelled down the ice flow and were dumped at the edge of the glacier. After temperatures returned to normal and the ice melted, the big sand pile

How it works: ice age

An ice age happens when the temperatures on the planet get so cold that glaciers cover the Earth. Over the last two million years, there have been four ice ages. Some glaciers start at the North Pole and spread south, and others start at the South Pole and spread north. If a plant or animal can't get used to the colder climate, it becomes extinct, and disappears forever. Sometimes, after the ice leaves, the shape of the land is different. Land that was once above water might now be below, and land that was once under water might now be above, like Sable Island. It's a game of ice age hide-and-seek!

From the air, Sable Island looks like nothing more than a sandbar.

was still there in the middle of the ocean. This pile was so high that some of it was above water, or sea level, and it formed an island—Sable Island.

Sable Island is very small. It's only forty-two kilometres long by one and a half kilometres wide—that's about as wide as two or three city blocks. In the city, it would take you about twenty minutes to walk that far, but on Sable Island, it would take you a lot longer because the sand is so deep. It's very tiring to walk in sand that deep.

A Shape-shifting Island

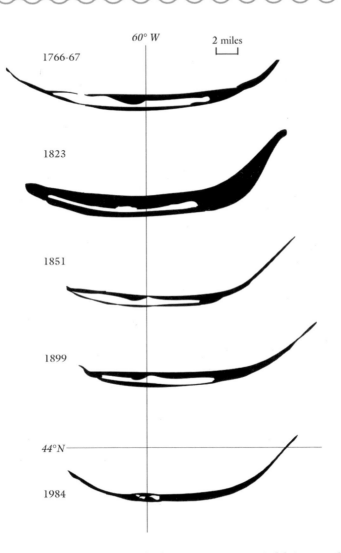

1766-67

1823

1851

1899

60° W

2 miles

44°N

1984

Strong winds and waves have eroded, or worn away, Sable's coastline over the years. This erosion, along with the constant movement of the sand by the wind, has changed the size and shape of Sable Island.

The wind and the waves are very strong on Sable Island. Together they move the sand around. Sometimes the sand is above water and sometimes it is below, which means the size and shape of Sable Island is always changing.

The wind mostly blows from the west side of the island, from the direction of Nova Scotia. This means that the sand is blown east, or away from Nova Scotia. Over hundreds of years, sand on the west side of the

Caught in the currents

Items from all over the world wash up on Sable Island because of the currents. It's not unusual to see a coconut on the beach even though the nearest coconut tree is over three thousand kilometres away. But coconuts aren't the only things coming in with the tide. According to Fisheries and Oceans Canada, a study of marine (ocean) litter in the 1980s showed that twenty thousand pieces of litter—mostly broken balloons—wash up on Sable Island's beaches every month, and over eighteen thousand of them are plastic.

In the water, a balloon or a plastic bag can look like a jellyfish. Animals can't digest plastic, so if an animal eats plastic, it will eventually die. Handfuls of small pieces of plastic—like plastic caps from pop bottles—are sometimes found in the stomachs of fish and birds after their deaths. Sometimes animals like seals drown when they are strangled by old fishing lines or balloon ribbons. Dolphins die of starvation after they get their snouts stuck in the plastic rings that hold together six-packs of canned pop.

island has been picked up by the wind, grain by grain, and blown to the east side. These small changes over long periods are changing how Sable Island looks on a map and sometimes it seems as if the island is moving slightly east!

Marine litter is a big problem on Sable Island, especially for the wildlife.

Ocean currents also play a part in shaping Sable Island. An ocean current is a large flow of water in a certain direction. Many things affect currents: the wind, the temperature of the air and the water, the shape of the ocean floor, and even the sun and the moon.

Sable Island is unique. It is caught in the middle of three ocean currents that come from three different directions. Some scientists believe that these three currents pushing against each other will keep Sable Island in place. Others wonder if Sable Island will someday disappear under the water again, forever.

Birds can't digest plastic. All that is left of this albatross is a few feathers, bones, and what was in his stomach when he died: a handful of plastic bottle caps.

Holding It All Together

The narrow North Beach and the wider, flat South Beach are separated by a row of sand dunes.

Sable Island has two beaches: North Beach runs along the north side of the island, and South Beach runs along the south side. The west and east ends of Sable Island each form a point, or what is called a sand spit.

The two beaches are separated by a row of sand

Now you see it, now you don't

The winds on Sable Island are so strong and there is so much sand being blown around that things often are buried—sometimes things as big as a house. One day during a storm, the bottom floor of the lightkeeper's house started filling up with sand. The lightkeeper and his family moved upstairs and went in and out through the windows. Eventually, the sand buried their whole house.

Sometimes, things that were buried show up again. A World War Two bomb was found on Sable Island—almost twenty years after the war ended. Maybe the lightkeeper's house will show up again someday, too!

dunes. Without the dunes, the island would be completely flat and maybe under water.

Dunes form when the waves pick up sand along the edge of the water and dump it onto the beach. Then the wind blows the sand around. If there is nothing to stop it, the sand just scatters all over the place; but if there is something like a shell or a clump of seaweed on the beach, a little pile of sand starts to form around it.

The waves and wind work together to add more and more sand to the pile until it is big enough to be called a dune. To keep the dune in place, however, it must have some vegetation.

You can see the roots of the marram grass in the "blowout" sections—sections of the dunes that have eroded, or broken apart.

Sable Island

Marram grass is a type of beach grass that grows well in sand. You have probably seen this grass at the beach. Marram starts to grow on top of the pile of sand. Every time the wind and waves add a new layer of sand, marram grows a new set of roots to hold it. The roots spread like a giant net, trapping the sand and keeping the dune in place.

"Wandering dunes" are sand dunes that don't have any plants to hold them in place. The wind scoops out sand from the front of the dune, and places it on top. Then the sand slowly slides down the back of

How it works: xerophytes

Marram grass is part of a plant family called "xerophytes" [zeer-uh-fights]. "Xero" means dry, and "phytes" means plants. A cactus is an example of a xerophyte that you might know. Xerophytes need little water. They grow well in dry and sandy places like beaches and deserts. These plants have special leaves that help the plant catch and keep water. If xerophytes couldn't store water, they'd dry out and die during the evaporation process, when the sun dries the water on their leaves and returns it to the atmosphere as vapour. A cactus has spines to do this job. Other xerophytes have scales or rolled leaves, like marram grass, and some even have even have a thick layer of hair on top of their leaves.

In August 2009, a wood and iron mast from a ship that probably wrecked on Sable Island hundreds of years ago appeared on South Beach just below the sand.

the dune, forming a new pile just behind the old spot. When this happens over and over, the dune appears to wander across the island.

It takes many years for a wandering dune to move, and as it moves, things that were once buried can suddenly reappear—even things that have been buried for hundreds of years, like items from shipwrecks.

Wandering dunes move in the same direction as the wind. Since the wind blows mostly from the west on Sable Island, the wandering dunes are slowly moving east. Eventually they will wander right off the island.

Hiking Bald Dune

There are currently three wandering dunes on Sable Island. Bald Dune is the largest. This naked dune is twenty-four metres high. That's as tall as an eight-floor building.

Over the last fifty years, Bald Dune has been slowly wandering from the northwest end of the island to the southeast end. Every year it gets closer to wandering right off Sable Island. Notice how Bald Dune looks like a desert compared to the dune at the bottom of the photo. That's because Bald Dune has no vegetation, like marram grass, to hold it in place. You can see the water on both sides of Sable Island from the top of Bald Dune, just by turning your head to the right and then to the left. When the weather is hot, the horses sometimes go up to the top of Bald Dune to catch a breeze. Or maybe they are going up for the view!

CHAPTER TWO

A Magical and Wild Place

The Magical

On Sable Island, the sand is magical—it "sings" when you walk on it. Singing sand is rare. It is found on some beaches and deserts as far away as Africa, Asia, and Europe, and as close to Sable Island as Prince Edward Island.

On Sable Island, the sand makes a squeaking noise that sounds like a small dog barking: "Yip, yip, yip." Some "sand-songs" sound like whistles, croaking frogs, and even burps.

Not all singing sand makes the same sound. It depends on the beach. On Sable Island, the sand makes a squeaking noise that sounds like a small dog barking: "Yip, yip, yip." Some "sand-songs" sound like whistles, croaking frogs, and even burps.

There are no rocks on Sable Island—not even little ones. Beach glass is rare, too, even though the waves bring hundreds of glass bottles onshore. The bottles

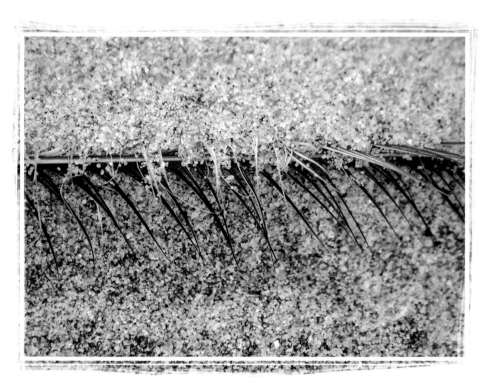

Sable Island sand is mostly made of quartz and the grains are the perfect shape for singing.

How it works: **singing sands**

When people walk on the sand, the weight of their feet pushing against the sand causes the grains to rub against each other. This rubbing makes a noise that sometimes sounds like singing. Singing sand is rare, because in order for sand to sing, everything must be just right. The sand must be really dry. The grains need to be round, smooth, and made of a type of mineral called quartz. Sable Island sand is almost all quartz, which makes it perfect for singing. You won't hear a peep out of singing sand, however, if it is wet or polluted.

don't break because there are no rocks. Sometimes empty bottles show up with notes sealed inside. And sometimes bottles wash up that have never been opened and are still full.

You won't find many seashells on Sable Island either. Only the largest creatures—like surf clams and moon snails—are strong enough to hold on to the ocean floor in the wild ocean currents. The moon snails on Sable Island are quite large and can grow up to seven inches around. One thing that you will find a lot of on Sable's beaches is animal bones, especially seal bones.

How it works: quicksand

Quicksand is just regular sand that is soaked with water. A patch of quicksand will often look like dry sand on top, but below that, there is water. When you step on a spot of quicksand, the water underneath quickly rushes to the top and mixes with the dry sand. This makes the sand watery, and because you can't stand on water, you start to sink. Don't worry; the quicksand won't swallow you whole like it does in comic books. You will probably only sink up to your knees.

The best thing to do if you ever find yourself stuck in quicksand is relax. The more you panic and struggle, the deeper you will sink. Remember, even though there is sand in quicksand, it is still water. You may not be able to walk on water, but you can float in it, so the best way to get out of quicksand is to lie back and float.

The Wild

Another kind of sand found on Sable Island is quicksand. Quicksand is a trickster. It's easy to be fooled by quicksand because it looks like normal sand, but if you step in a patch, you could get stuck. It won't be singing and neither will you!

Sable Island is the foggiest place in Atlantic Canada. The island gets up to 127 days of fog every year. The fog is caused by two of the ocean currents that meet at Sable Island. When the cold water of the northern Labrador Current mixes with the warm water of the southern Gulf Stream, a heavy fog is created.

The thick fog and the

Fog days according to Environment Canada's 2001 "Weather Winners" study:

City	Days of Fog
Whitehorse, YT	14
Montreal, QC	16
Yellowknife, NT	18
Saskatoon, SK	20
Calgary, AB	21
Vancouver, BC	23
Toronto, ON	27
Charlottetown, PE	43
Moncton, NB	51
Halifax, NS	99
St. John's, NL	118
Sable Island	127

Sable Island is more than just sand. In the summer the dunes and valleys are alive with colour.

strong ocean currents add to the danger in the waters surrounding Sable Island. That and the sharks!

More Than Just Sand

There's more than just sand on Sable Island; otherwise the wildlife there could not survive. Almost half of Sable Island is covered in vegetation. Grasses, flowers, and low bushes like cranberry and blueberry grow on the ridges of dunes between North Beach and South Beach.

Because of the strong winds and blowing sands, the vegetation doesn't grow very high. That's why there are no trees on Sable Island— well, except one. In the last hundred years, over eighty thousand trees were planted, but only one survived.

In the last hundred years, over eighty thousand trees were planted, but only one survived.

The "Sable Island National Forest"

This sturdy little Scots Pine is the only tree on Sable Island. Tens of thousands of trees have been planted over the years, but only this one survived. Strong winds and blowing sand keep this tree from growing to its full size. Even though it is over forty years old, it looks more like a bush than a tree. As a joke, the people who live on Sable Island call this tree the "Sable Island National Forest."

Wildlife can't survive without water, either. Even though Sable Island is surrounded by water, it is ocean water, and is too salty to drink. Luckily, Sable Island has many freshwater ponds.

Seals lying in the warm summer sun next to Lake Wallace.

Also, within the sand, there is an aquifer. When the horses can't find fresh water on land, they will use their front feet to dig a watering hole. In the winter, when the ponds are frozen, the horses will eat snow if they are thirsty.

On South Beach, there is a large body of water called Lake Wallace. At one time, the lake was so deep that the people who lived on Sable Island could swim in it and sail boats on it. Now it is too shallow to do those things. Like a lot of things on Sable Island, Lake Wallace is filling in with sand.

Lake Wallace is no longer fresh water, either. Sable's coastline has eroded, or broken down, over the years and now the ocean is much closer to the lake. During storms, the waves splash into the lake, making it too salty to drink.

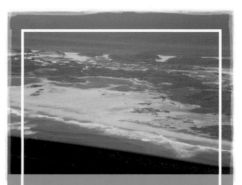

Sable Island is more than just sand

This is a photo of South Beach taken from an airplane. Notice the summer vegetation and all the freshwater ponds. If you look closely, you can see some horses having a drink in the pond area. The largest body of water is Lake Wallace. Notice how close it is to the ocean. The Sable Island Station is in the top left-hand corner and "Main Street"— what the locals call this road through the sand as a joke— is to the right of the station.

CHAPTER THREE

The Wildlife of Sable Island

Sharks, Seals, and Sponges

The wildlife on Sable Island is special. Some birds nest only on Sable Island, nowhere else. A little sea sponge that grows in Lake Wallace is not found anywhere else in the world. An orchid is a very rare flower, but on Sable Island there are many different types of this flower.

Seals sunbathing on South Beach. Fifty thousand grey seals live year round on Sable Island—that's more than anywhere else in the world.

This seal was probably a victim of a shark attack. Its body, baked in the summer sun, provides a meal for a hungry bird.

A few hundred harbour seals and fifty thousand grey seals live on Sable Island year round. More grey seals live here than in any other place in the world.

The seals like to bodysurf in the giant waves around Sable Island. This can be dangerous, because sharks kill a few hundred seals every year. There are eighteen kinds of sharks (including the great white shark) in the waters around Sable Island. There are also many species of whales and dolphins in the area.

In the olden days, people brought animals like rabbits, cows, sheep, and pigs to Sable Island. None of those animals live there today. Some were eaten by humans, and some were eaten by each other.

There are eighteen kinds of sharks (including the great white shark) in the waters around Sable Island.

Walruses once lived on Sable Island, too. They were hunted until there were none left. Hunters killed them for their meat and their ivory tusks, which are very valuable. Sometimes you can find walrus bones in the sand, even though walruses have not been on Sable Island for over one hundred and fifty years.

Many birds migrate to Sable Island during spring and summer. Migratory birds, or birds that come from other parts of the world, stop at Sable to eat or have babies. Sable Island is a migratory bird sanctuary.

Terns sometimes lay their eggs in nests on the beach. Nests aren't something terns spend a lot of time building—notice that these twigs aren't formed into a traditional nest.

This means that the government protects the birds that land on the island.

Some birds fly to Sable Island on purpose and return every year. Other birds are blown onto the island by mistake. Birds from as far away as New Zealand and South America have shown up on Sable Island during storms.

One of the largest groups of roseate terns in Canada nests on Sable Island. Roseate terns have tail feathers that look like a fork, but with two prongs instead of four. These noisy little birds will dive-bomb you if you get too close to their nests. They can glide under water for a short time when they are chasing food, and when they mate, the male tern flies in circles in the sky with a fish to attract the females.

The Ipswich sparrow is found in other places along the Atlantic coast, but Sable Island is the only place in the world that this tiny songbird nests. Both the roseate terns and Ipswich sparrows are being closely watched in Canada because these birds are at risk of disappearing forever.

The Famous Sable Island Horses

Sable Island is most famous for its wild horses. There are two hundred to four hundred horses living there. No one is exactly sure how the horses got on the island. People

There are between two hundred and four hundred wild horses living on Sable Island. This one is enjoying some flowers unconcerned by the human nearby.

The Deportation of the Acadians

The Acadians are a French-speaking people who first settled in Nova Scotia over four hundred years ago. In the 1700s England ruled Nova Scotia and was at war with France. The Acadians didn't want to fight in the war. They said they were on England's side but England didn't trust them, so in 1755, England deported, or sent away, the Acadians. They took the Acadians' money, land, and animals and put the Acadians on ships and sent them to the United States and Europe. Several thousand Acadians died during the deportation. After the war, many Acadians returned to their homes, but their land and possessions had been given away.

Acadian horses are different from other horses. They are quite sturdy and have short legs. They also have tiny ears that tip towards each other. Most people think that Sable Island's most famous animals are ponies because of their size, but they are horses.

used to think that they survived a shipwreck and swam to shore. Now most believe that a Boston ship owner, Thomas Hancock, put the horses there— horses he took from the Acadian people during the Deportation in 1755. No one is sure why Hancock put the horses on Sable Island, but he never went back for them.

The horses were tame when they were dropped off on the island. Without any humans around, they quickly went back to their wild ways and formed herds. Each herd, or band, has four to eight horses. The most dominant, or strongest, male horse leads and defends the family band. He is called the stallion. The rest of the band is made up of a couple of other male horses, some mares (female horses), and their babies, or foals.

Acadian horses have tiny ears that tip towards each other.

Young male horses that are not part of a family band often form "bachelor bands." Sometimes the horses from a bachelor band will fight the stallion of a family band for his mares. Older male horses often travel alone, or become "tags." They are called this

Sometimes horses from other bands will fight a stallion for his mares.

because they tag along with a family band but stay a short distance away from them.

There are about fifty herds on Sable Island, and they each have their own home range, or area. The bands will cross through each other's ranges, but the horses usually don't mix.

No horses allowed

Horses clean, scratch, and "comb" each other's coats by using their teeth. This is called grooming. Horses also "auto-groom"—clean and scratch themselves—by rolling in wet sand or by rubbing their bodies against things like driftwood and fences. The horses used to rub themselves against expensive weather equipment used at the Sable Island Station, as well as some of the buildings. This behaviour damaged both the equipment and the buildings so the government put up a fence around the station area to keep the horses out.

A Cat Nap

Can you tell which horse is sleeping? Horses can sleep standing up. If we go to sleep while we're standing, we fall over as soon as our muscles relax. But horses can lock their legs so this won't happen. They have special bones and muscles in their legs called a "stay apparatus." Horses can sleep lying down, too, but because they are so large, it takes them a long time to get up. If there is danger, a horse can run away faster if it is already standing. Plus, horses are so heavy that the weight of their bodies can hurt their insides if they are lying down for too long. Horses aren't the only animals that can sleep standing up. Elephants and giraffes do it too. (Oh, and it's the black horse sleeping here!)

It's a Hard Life

Life on Sable Island can be hard for the horses. There's no shelter from the wind or blowing sand, or from anything really. The winters on Sable Island are milder than on the mainland. Sable gets more rain than snow in the winter and the horses can get quite soggy and cold. Sometimes, the weaker horses—the very young, or the very old—don't live through the winter. Older

Notice the teeth in this horse's skull. They are worn down and broken because the horse chewed too much sand with its food.

horses can starve to death because they can no longer chew their food. Sand gets in everything the horses eat and eventually it wears down their teeth.

The Sable horses grow thick woolly coats in the winter to stay warm. This horse is losing his winter coat.

Sable Island

A Sable Island horse is being lifted into a ship to be taken to the mainland.

Even though the Sable Island horses have no predators, at one time humans were their enemies. In the past, whenever the government decided there were too many horses on Sable Island, they would catch some of them and ship them to the mainland. The horses were scared and often got hurt during the capture. If they survived the long trip across the ocean, they didn't have a happy ending. Some went to zoos or to the coal mines of Cape Breton, Nova Scotia, as

[___] Lorette Avenue
Winnipeg 9, Manitoba
June 15, 1960

Dear John Diefenbaker,

I like horse very much. I am grateful for what you did for the Sable Island ponies. I sure hope that you will have a man there to take care of the ponies. Will the hay be bought by boat or plane?

Last winter my class went to the parliament building in Winnipeg. We saw the men in session as we sat in the balcony.

We also saw the star that was in the middle of a big room. If you went up two floors there is a big circle with a fence around it. If you looked down you would see the star in the opposite direction.

Your friend,
Heidi [___]

P.S.
This letter is strictly for you, not for your secretary.

Kids *can* make a difference. When it was reported that the Sable Island horses were facing death, Canadian schoolchildren wrote hundreds of letters like these to save the horses.

Sable Island

**** Boyd Avenue
Winnipeg 4, Manitoba
June 15, 1960

Dear Sirs,

I heard about you saving the horses on Sable Island from being sold. The ponies would have probably ended up being fed to my dog. Those ponies deserve to be as free as the wind because they didn't harm us so why should we harm them. Thank you for saving them from death.

I like animals and I always try to help them if they are in trouble. I am a Smokey the Bear Junior Forest Ranger and I always try to prevent fires when I am out camping.

In Manitoba, we have many natural wonders. I hope, someday, you will be able to come to Manitoba to see our scenery.

I am in grade six and twelve years old. Could you please write a letter back?

    Sincerely,
    Daniel Mordehi

Lightning

workhorses. Others were sent to factories where they were killed and their body parts were made into dog food or glue.

All this changed in 1959 when it was reported in the newspaper that the government was going to get rid of all the horses on Sable Island and that they would most likely be destroyed and be made into dog food or glue. Once again, the horses were facing death. Animal lovers everywhere were upset. Schoolchildren from across Canada wrote hundreds of letters to the prime minister at the time, John George Diefenbaker, asking him to save the Sable Island horses.

Canada's Thirteenth Prime Minister

When John George Diefenbaker was eight years old, he told his mother that he would be prime minister one day—and he was, from 1957 to 1963.

Diefenbaker did more than just save the Sable Island horses. He passed the Canadian Bill of Rights, which gave Canadians freedom of speech and freedom of religion, and passed a law giving Aboriginals, or native people, the right to vote.

Sable Island

How to start a letter-writing campaign

With the help of a teacher or parent, look on the Internet to find the name and address of the person and organization that you want to write to. Tell everyone you know what you are doing. Ask your friends, family, classmates, school, and even your community to help you by sending their own letters. The more letters you send the better chance you have of getting what you want.

Here are some tips to help you write a great letter:

· Keep your letter short and polite

· Say who you are

· Explain why you are writing

· Tell the person or organization what you would like done

· Provide your contact information so you may receive an answer (make sure you check with your teacher or parents first before giving out this information)

· Give a cut-off date and say that you will be in touch again by this date if you don't receive an answer

· Be sure to express your thanks

The Wildlife of Sable Island

No help allowed

It is against the law for anyone to feed, touch, or even help the wild horses of Sable Island. This male horse has one leg that is longer than his other three and a foot that is shaped like the base of a rocking chair. He walks slowly with a limp and has a hard time keeping up with his band. His band looks out for him, though, stopping every now and then so he can catch up to them.

Diefenbaker was an animal lover too, and in June 1960, he passed a law that would protect the horses for as long as there was a government station on Sable Island. Once again, hundreds of letters from schoolchildren poured into the prime minister's office to thank him. The Sable Island horses have been protected ever since.

Circle of life

On Sable Island, everything returns to nature and becomes part of something else. Horse dung, or droppings, is perfect for a village of dung beetles that live under mushroom umbrellas, and this skeleton is all that remains of a dead horse that would have been a feast for the many birds on Sable Island.

CHAPTER FOUR

Sable's Wild Past—
Pirates, Shipwrecks & Ghosts

Early Settlers

Sable Island was discovered five hundred years ago but up until a couple of hundred years ago, no one really lived on the island. Some tried, but travelling to Sable Island was dangerous. Back then, the only way to get to the island was by ship. Fog, storms, currents, and hidden sandbars that stretch for miles underneath the water caused many shipwrecks.

If you landed safely on Sable Island, you then had to survive the island and its wild storms. Sometimes the weather prevented the supply ships from the mainland from getting to Sable Island. When that happened the settlers had to eat what they could find on the island, which was not much. Most people found it too hard to live on the island and returned to the mainland.

Many people who landed on Sable Island ended up there by accident. Ships travelling between North America and Europe had to sail right by Sable Island. There were lots of fishing boats in the area too, as the waters were full of fish. Hundreds of ships and fishing boats passed by Sable Island every year, and many just ran into the island by mistake.

Sable Island was once home to a group of convicts, or prisoners. It was a good place for prisoners, because they couldn't escape. The prisoners were part of a plan to build a new settlement in the "New World"—America. The prisoners were left on the island while others in charge went to look for a good place to settle. They didn't go back for the prisoners, though. It was years before a ship picked them up and by then, only a few were alive. Most had starved to death.

Sailing safely through dangerous waters

Hundreds of years ago, captains used "sextants" to safely navigate, or steer their ships through dangerous waters. A sextant used the position of the sun or the stars to figure out where a ship was in the ocean. Sextants could not be used if it was foggy or cloudy because they couldn't see the sun or the stars; and Sable Island was often hidden in a thick fog.

Captains also used "dead reckoning" to navigate. Dead reckoning was really just a guess based on how fast the ship was going, and how far it had already travelled. Christopher Columbus was said to be good at dead reckoning and he used it during his famous voyages to the Americas.

Dead reckoning, or even sextants, didn't always work. Sometimes no matter how careful a captain was, stormy seas and strong winds could blow the ship into Sable Island anyway.

When the ships came closer, they wrecked on the sandbars and then the pirates robbed and murdered the people on the ships.

Sable Island was also home to pirates at one time. The pirates would trick passing ships into coming closer to the island by pretending to be in trouble. When the ships came closer, they wrecked on the sandbars and then the pirates robbed and murdered the people on the ships.

The Graveyard of the Atlantic

There have been over 350 shipwrecks on Sable Island since they started keeping records, and thousands of people have drowned. The area around Sable Island is called the "Graveyard of the Atlantic" because once a ship wrecks, Sable's strong winds and waves bury it in the sand. An entire ship can disappear overnight!

Sable Island

Wrecked on a sandbar, this ship (the *Gale*) is almost buried in sand.

The area around Sable is called the "Graveyard of the Atlantic" because once a ship wrecks, Sable's strong winds and waves bury it in the sand.

Many "wreckers" lived on Sable Island, too. Wreckers are people who steal valuables from shipwrecks. By the early 1800s, stories of robberies and the murders of passengers from ships that had wrecked on Sable

Island were beginning to reach the mainland. It was time for the government to do something.

Saving Lives

In 1801, the government sent people to live on Sable Island. Their main reason for being there was to set up a lifesaving station to help the survivors of shipwrecks. The government also hoped that having people living on the island year round would keep the pirates and wreckers away.

Five buildings were built in different places on the island. Food, firewood,

The lifesaving crew practised rowing both on land and in the water.

and a map to the main station house were left in each building.

A group of men was put in charge of lifesaving. They worked hard and practised rowing their boat every day—both on land and in the water. They needed to be ready to fight the giant waves and the strong currents during a rescue. The lifesaving crew was very brave. It was dangerous work and over the years they saved hundreds of people from drowning.

In the late 1800s, two lighthouses were built to help prevent shipwrecks. East Light was built on the east

Saving lives

The lifesaving crew used a "Lyle" gun and "breeches buoy" to save shipwreck survivors. The Lyle gun looked like a cannon, but instead of shooting cannon balls, it shot a line out to the sinking ship. This allowed shipwreck survivors to be pulled to safety by a pulley system similar to a clothesline. Sometimes they attached the breeches buoy to the line. A breeches buoy was like a big pair of pants, or shorts, attached to a life preserver. A person would get into the buoy, and then the crew would pull them to safety. It was kind of like a zip line.

There are no lighthouse keepers on Sable Island anymore. Lighthouses, like the West Light above, are now automatic.

end of the island, and West Light on the west end. The lighthouses had many problems. Strong winds and waves eroded land at both ends of the island. East Light had to be moved and rebuilt three times, and West Light eight times.

In the olden days, lighthouse keepers looked after the lighthouses. They had to stay awake all night to make

Not so merry

This is all that is left of the *Merrimac*. The rest of it is buried in the sand on South Beach. The *Merrimac* left the United States for a trip across the Atlantic Ocean and wrecked on the Sable sandbars during a storm in July 1999. Luckily, no one was hurt. The *Merrimac* was the last shipwreck on Sable Island. Before this happened, there had not been a shipwreck on the island for over fifty years.

How it works: **radar**

Have you ever shouted into a canyon, or even an empty house, and heard your voice echo back? When you shout, you are sending out sound waves. When those waves hit something, like the walls of the canyon or the empty house, they bounce back to you and you hear your voice echoing back. A ship's radar works almost the same way—except that instead of sound waves, it uses invisible radio waves or microwaves to help the ship avoid dangers in the water like sandbars.

Radar, which stands for Radio Detection and Ranging, also measures the time it takes for the radio waves to bounce back. That tells the ship's captain how close an object is. It can even tell how fast the object is going, which is why police use radar to catch speeders. Radar is also used by air traffic controllers to direct airplanes, as well as in automatic doors that slide open as you walk towards them.

sure the lights didn't go out. Today, the Sable Island lighthouses are automatic—no humans needed.

Once the lighthouses were built, there were fewer shipwrecks on Sable Island. And, with the invention of radar, ships were able to avoid dangerous areas and there were fewer accidents. In 1958, after eleven years without a shipwreck on Sable Island, the life-saving station closed.

A Haunted Place

Many people died on Sable Island and Sable's wild history includes a few ghost stories:

Mrs. Copeland's Wedding Ring

Mrs. Copeland was travelling on a ship called the Frances, when it shipwrecked on Sable Island. Wreckers cut off Mrs. Copeland's ring finger to steal her wedding ring. No one knows if Mrs. Copeland was dead or alive when her ring was stolen but many have claimed to see her ghost at night walking on the beach. She is wet and crying and dripping blood from her left hand, which is missing its ring finger.

The 13th Oarsman

One of Sable Island's brave lifesaving crew died from an injury. He was an oarsman who rowed the lifesaving boat. Before he died, he said he would come back, and he did. According to stories, the "13th Oarsman," as he was called, always appeared in the lifeboat whenever there was a rescue.

Connecting to the rest of the world

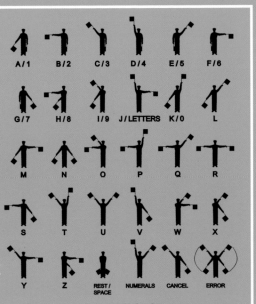

The semaphore alphabet

In the past, people living on Sable Island didn't have telephones or mail to connect to the rest of the world. If there was an emergency, it could take months or even years to get a message to the mainland by ship. A faster way had to be found. They tried training pigeons to carry messages but most of the pigeons didn't make it. They either died during the long ocean trip or were eaten by predators.

Telegraphs were also used on Sable Island as a way to send messages. A telegraph operator sends messages by radio, tapping out sounds using Morse code. It's a bit like texting. When you text, the numbers on your phone stand for letters of the alphabet. With Morse code, instead of numbers, you use dots and dashes to make the letters and words. For example, "SOS" is a signal that means "help." To send an SOS signal, you tap a letter "s" which is three dots in a row, then an "o" which is three dashes, followed by another "s". So "SOS" in Morse code looks like: ...---...

The people on Sable Island also used semaphore to send messages to passing ships. Semaphore uses flags to send signals. Letters and words are formed depending on how the person holds the two semaphore flags. Semaphore only works if you can see the person that you are signalling.

CHAPTER FIVE

Sable Island Today

Living on Sable Island

Lifesaving is no longer the main job of the people who live and work on Sable Island. Except for the *Merrimac*, there have been no shipwrecks in over sixty years. Today, the Sable Island Station mainly collects weather and climate information—something it has been doing for over one hundred years.

Only five or six people live on Sable Island year round. One is a naturalist, and the others work for the government collecting weather and climate data.

The Sable Island Station today. Visitors can pay to stay at the staff house— the large white building with the brick chimney

More people live on Sable Island during the summer. Some of them are seasonal workers who mow the grass around the station and paint buildings. Scientists also visit the island in the summer. Like Zoe Lucas (see sidebar), they want to study the island and its wildlife.

The Sable Island Station has many buildings. There are work buildings, garages, storage areas, and homes. The people who live on Sable Island year round have their own homes. The seasonal workers and the visiting scientists live in the "staff house."

Visitors to Sable Island must pay to stay at the staff

Zoe Lucas examines a dead horse

Zoe Lucas is a researcher and naturalist who studies the island and its wildlife. Zoe first went to Sable Island in 1971 as a university student, fell in love with the island, and eventually made it her home. Zoe has lived on Sable Island for about thirty years and is an expert on the Sable Island horses. Zoe also runs a website called the *Sable Island Green Horse Society* which is all about Sable Island.

A powerful idea

The Sable Island Station needs to be self-sufficient, just in case it gets cut off from the rest of Nova Scotia. That is one reason why the Sable Island Station makes as much of its own power as possible. The station wants to use power that is healthier for the environment so it uses the sun and wind to make power. Sable Island gets less sun than the rest of Nova Scotia so it can't make enough solar power to run the whole station, but as the windiest place in the province, it is perfect for a wind farm.

house, but it is not like a hotel. Everyone has chores to do and visitors must bring their own food from the mainland and make their own meals. Bathrooms, and sometimes even bedrooms, have to be shared depending on how many visitors are at the house. And you even have to bring your own pillow and sleeping bag. Don't expect room service here!

There is no garbage dump on Sable Island. Visitors must take all their garbage with them when they leave the island. Some of the garbage from the Sable Island Station is burned. The rest is sent to the mainland by airplane. This gives a whole new meaning to the idea of air mail!

Once a year, a ship delivers supplies to Sable Island. The ship must anchor off shore because there are no wharves or docks on the island. A helicopter transports the supplies from the ship to the island in a giant net called a sling.

Driving on Sable Island

The people on Sable Island drive trucks and all-terrain vehicles (ATVs) to get around the island. The trucks have wide rubber tires to make it easier to drive in the deep sand. They try not to stop their vehicles on the beach because when they do, they sometimes get stuck. On Sable Island you are only allowed to drive on the beach and nowhere else. Sometimes this is difficult if the tide is high and water blocks the way. If you drive on wet areas, you could sink. Driving on the dunes, or in areas where wildlife is nesting, is not allowed.

A helicopter transporting supplies from the supply ship to Sable Island during the annual sea-lift.

Sable Island gets its fuel and most of its food from the supply ship. If the weather is too stormy or foggy, the "sea-lift," as they call it, can't happen and they will have to wait another year for the ship to come back. They need to have extra supplies on hand, just in case this happens.

Sable Island can get supplies in between the sea-lifts, if needed. Every two weeks, depending on the weather, a plane from Halifax brings fresh food (mostly fruits and vegetables) along with the mail. Sable Island is not as cut off from the mainland as it was a hundred years ago: telephones and the Internet now connect Sable Island to the rest of the world.

Visiting Sable Island

Streets of Sand: The people who live on Sable call this area "Main Street, Sable Island" as a joke.

In order to visit Sable Island, you must write to the Canadian Coast Guard for permission. Only fifty to one hundred people are allowed to visit the island each year, and most of those people are scientists.

There are two ways to get to Sable Island—by boat or by airplane. Both are expensive and both can be affected by the weather.

It takes about twenty-four hours to get to Sable Island from Halifax by ship. There are no wharves on Sable, and the ships can't get close to the island because of the sandbars and currents, so they must put down their anchors in the deep water offshore and bring people to the island by motorboat. This doesn't always work: Over the last thirty years, fourteen cruise ships have tried to get to Sable Island, but only four have made it. The other ten had to turn back because of the fog.

Over the last thirty years, fourteen cruise ships have tried to get to Sable Island, but only four have made it. The other ten had to turn back because of the fog.

It is not much easier to travel by airplane. The fog often prevents planes from getting to Sable Island, too. There is only one plane that flies to Sable Island and it leaves from Halifax. The plane is only big enough for five people plus the pilot. Because it is so small, it can't carry very much so everything must be weighed before it goes onboard—including you.

This six-seater plane is used for flights to Sable Island because it has large tires, which are better for landing on sand, and it only needs a short distance to land and to take off.

It takes about an hour and a half to two hours to get from Halifax to Sable Island by plane, depending on the wind. It is very noisy onboard and passengers must wear headphones to block out the sound of the engines. Life jackets must be worn at all times while on the plane and it is suggested that you wear a survival suit. A survival suit is a waterproof suit that will help you stay dry if the plane goes down over the ocean. The suit will protect you from the cold, but not from anything that might be in the water. No meal on this flight, except maybe for the sharks!

The Sable Island "Airport"

There is no runway on Sable Island; the planes land right on the beach. Before every flight to Sable, the Halifax airport checks with the Sable Island station manager to make sure the weather is clear, and that there is a safe spot to land.

There are only a few spots on the island where a plane can land safely. When the island is expecting a plane, the station manager drives to a landing spot and makes

The Sable Island "runway"—sand as far as you can see.

This seal is lying across the deep grooves made by the wide tires of the station truck, using the edge of the track as a pillow.

sure it is still safe and that it didn't wash out during an overnight storm. If it did, a new spot must be found.

A good place for a runway is anywhere there is enough room. It must be away from the water and the ground needs to be solid. Once the station manager finds a spot, any driftwood or garbage is cleared from the area. The station manager then drives the station truck back and forth, over and over, to make sure the ground is firm.

To make sure that the runway is long enough for the plane to land safely, the station manager measures the distance by using the truck's odometer. If everything is okay, the station manager calls the airport and gives the plane permission to take off. There's a very good chance that there might be a horse on the runway that will need to be moved before the plane can land!

There is no control tower or air traffic controller to help the pilot land the plane. The pilot must find the runway with the help of the station manager who is waiting by the runway. The station manager helps

The station manager must move any horses from the runway before a plane can land.

Sable Island

the pilot see the runway from the air by placing giant brightly coloured rubber balls beside the runway. The pilot also looks for the tire tracks that the station

The windsock on the bumper of the station manager's truck tells the pilot which way the wind is blowing and the rubber balls will be placed in the sand to show where the runway is.

manager has made with the station truck while driving back and forth over the runway spot.

The station manager sticks a windsock on the bumper of the truck. A windsock looks like a giant red-and-white striped sock. When the wind blows, it fills the sock with air and the sock blows in the same direction as the wind. This tells the pilot which way the wind is blowing, which is important for landing the plane safely. The station manager also lights a flare to signal the pilot.

The Sable Island horses will continue to be protected by Parks Canada.

The Future of Sable Island

The Canadian Coast Guard has protected Sable Island since 1867—since the birth of Canada. In May 2010, it was announced that protection of the island will be handed over to Parks Canada and Sable Island will become a national park. Parks Canada has a long history of caring for Canada's most beautiful places and the hope is that they will continue to protect this wild and magical island.

Want to learn more?

To learn more about Sable Island, visit:

The Maritime Museum of the Atlantic, Halifax, Nova Scotia
www.museum.gov.ns.ca/mmanew

The Nova Scotia Museum of Natural History, Halifax, Nova Scotia
www.museum.gov.ns.ca/mnhnew

The *Sable Island Green Horse Society* website
www.greenhorsesociety.com

Acknowledgements

Thanks to Gerry Forbes, Rick Welsford, and especially Zoe Lucas for sharing their knowledge of Sable Island; David Carter of the Nova Scotia Museum of Natural History, Cheryl Avery of the University of Saskatchewan, Jeanne Gallagher of Algalita Marine Research Foundation, Sable Island Preservation Trust, Lynn-Marie Richard and Dan Conlin of the Maritime Museum of the Atlantic, and especially Sharon Irving Kennedy for photos; Mark Finnamore, Sarah Cain Henwood, Colleen Kitts, and especially Wesley Doherty for writing and editing guidance; and the Nimbus Publishing team of Penelope Jackson, Kate Kennedy, Patrick Murphy, and Heather Bryan.

Glossary

aquifer:	the space holding a layer of water beneath the ground
beacon:	a light or other visible signal for warning or guiding
bodysurf:	to ride the crest of a wave without using a surfboard
climate:	the temperature and weather conditions of an area over time
current:	a flow of water (or air) moving in a certain direction
erosion:	wearing away of the earth's surface by wind or water
glaciers:	large sheets of ice that remain solid even in the summer
lightkeeper:	a person who is responsible for looking after a lighthouse and its light
migrate:	to move from one place to another

naturalist: a person who studies the plants and animals living in a region

odometer: an instrument that measures distance travelled

predator: an animal that naturally preys on (or eats) other animals

radar: (short for Radio Detection and Ranging) detects where an object is and how fast it is moving by measuring the time it takes for radio waves to bounce back

sanctuary: an area set aside for birds or other animals, and protected by law

sandbar: a large bank of sand that forms in an ocean or river

sand dune: a large ridge of sand formed by the wind

self-sufficient: able to survive without outside help or materials

vapour: water or other liquids in gas form

vegetation: the plants growing on an area of land

Text Sources

Much of the information contained in this text was a result of conversations with Zoe Lucas, Independent Researcher and Naturalist, and Gerry Forbes, Sable Island Station Manager (Environment Canada) while visiting Sable Island.

Other text sources include:

Appleton, Thomas E. *USQUE AD MARE, A History of the Canadian Coast Guard and Marine Services (Sable Island)*
www.ccg-gcc.gc.ca/eng/CCG/USQUE_Sable_Island

Bertin, Johanna. *Sable Island: Tales of Tragedy and Survival from the Graveyard of the Atlantic*, Altitude Publishing, 2006

Beson, Kevin. *Towards a Conservation Strategy for Sable Island*, Environment Canada's Canadian Wildlife Service, Atlantic Region.
www.ns.ec.gc.ca/reports/sable.html

The Canadian Encyclopedia
www.thecanadianencyclopedia.com

Fisheries and Oceans Canada
www.nfl.dfo-mpo.gc.ca/e0011139

Hinterland Who's Who
www.hww.ca/hww2.asp?id=69

How Stuff Works
www.science.howstuffworks.com

The Maritime Museum of the Atlantic
www.museum.gov.ns.ca/mmanew

National Climate Data and Information Archive (Environment
Canada)
www.climate.weatheroffice.gc.ca/winners/categorydata_
e.html?SelectedCategory=38

The Nova Scotia Museum of Natural History
www.museum.gov.ns.ca/mnhnew

Parks Canada, Sable Island
www.pc.gc.ca/eng/progs/np-pn/cnpn-cnnp/sable/
nature.aspx

The Sable Island Green Horse Society
www.greenhorsesociety.com

The Sable Island Preservation Trust
www.sabletrust.ns.ca

Image Sources

All photos courtesy of Wendy Kitts except:

Sharon Irving Kennedy: pages vi, 2, 4, 16, 23, 25, 28, 30, 34, 41, 45, 63, 72, 74, 81

Rick Welsford, Sable Island Preservation Trust: pages 5, 13, 37, 42, 43, 77, 80

Maritime Museum of the Atlantic: pages 47, 55, 59, 61

Nova Scotia Museum of Natural History: page 17

University of Saskatchewan Archives (JG Diefenbaker fonds, 1960–1962.): pages 48, 49

Algalita Marine Research Foundation: page 15

Nimbus Publishing: pages 8, 11

Harper's Magazine, December 1866: page 54

Scribner's Magazine, Volume 19: page 62